Everything
Reminds
You of
Something
Else

ESSENTIAL POETS SERIES 240

**Canada Council Conseil des Arts
for the Arts du Canada**

ONTARIO ARTS COUNCIL
CONSEIL DES ARTS DE L'ONTARIO

an Ontario government agency
un organisme du gouvernement de l'Ontario

Canadä

Guernica Editions Inc. acknowledges the support of the Canada Council
for the Arts and the Ontario Arts Council. The Ontario Arts Council
is an agency of the Government of Ontario.

We acknowledge the financial support of the Government of Canada.
Nous reconnaissons l'appui financier du gouvernement du Canada.

Everything Reminds You of Something Else

ELANA WOLFF

GUERNICA
EDITIONS
TORONTO • BUFFALO • LANCASTER (U.K.)
2017

Michael Mirolla, editor
David Moratto, cover and interior design
Guernica Editions Inc.
1569 Heritage Way, Oakville, (ON), Canada L6M 2Z7
2250 Military Road, Tonawanda, N.Y. 14150-6000 U.S.A.
www.guernicaeditions.com

Distributors:
University of Toronto Press Distribution,
5201 Dufferin Street, Toronto (ON), Canada M3H 5T8
Gazelle Book Services, White Cross Mills
High Town, Lancaster LA1 4XS U.K.

First edition.
Printed in Canada.

Legal Deposit—First Quarter
Library of Congress Catalog Card Number: 2016952729
Library and Archives Canada Cataloguing in Publication
Wolff, Elana, author
Everything reminds you of something else / Elana Wolff. -- First edition.
(Essential poets series ; 240)
Poems.
ISBN 978-1-77183-189-5 (paperback)
I. Title. II. Series: Essential poets series ; 240
PS8595.O5924E94 2017   C811'.54   C2016-905967-7

For Menachem

Contents

"Your anxiety … I see in it a lack of necessary faith."
—Franz Kafka, *The Trial*

"Everything resembled something else.
Everything was connected to something else."
—Roberto Calasso, *Ka*

"And the one who lives in secret / abides in the shade."
—A. F. Moritz, *Sequence*

Jerusalem Day

First commandment: drown and all is water.

They pull me from the lake ~

fish-slippery ~ grappling at the raft.

White jelly-legs, amphibian feet.

Tongue as slow as Moses'. Cold. We laugh

but I am gasping, clothed & drawn from water.

I'm the pike who swallowed the frog, the frog

who died for science. I'm the guy so wise

he had his uterus removed; the maid who climbed

inside it, mute as math. I'm the child—the copula

to be / betwixt / the link. *Anyhow*

life gets into our lungs. It's trust that has to bristle up.

The Bower

The village has a pond,
it has a bower.
The pond is broad and shallow,
the bower small and lower—

hidden in the valley
from traffic in the street.
Its face as firm as faith,
its back an even sheath—

from equinox to equinox.
This is when it draws
you down and when
the bond is strongest.

The pond is there for those
who want the mirroring
of water: world & self
reflected back in image.

The bower is a cover
for a secrecy that deepens.
Lie beneath the over-
lapping boughs

and climbing vines.
To form you are a supine
mind: to mind
you are idea.

A bird is picking glitter
from a twig above your head.
You used to do that as a child: pick twigs
and glitter, hide your little treasures

in a box. The box was found,
the top removed; they'd outlived
their objective. Glitter
and the twigs retain their mystery.

The village has a pond,
it has a bower.

The Tower

At first there was the brain-grey plane.
Warmth arose

as cover. Context dawned elliptically and swiftly: tower,
town:
the intersect of upright/horizontal, portrait/
ground.

Light replaced the anvil with a silver wingtip-touch,
a fluency of flutes.

Outwardly, I'm drawn toward the swath of corn-pone gold.
Here there could be anything—
all the mirth of rose un-
folding mauve
in perfect birth.

Inwardly, I'm focused on the sliver—
gun-grey blue:
the tower, and the old familiar sequence it reflects:

reach and freeze,

block and dodge.

Fey   and fade away.

The soul slips into the hidden oubliette.

The Bestiary

Long before speech was achieved, the elephant held memory.

The dog embodied the sad devout,
                                    the mouse—the dutiful doubtful.

Conjugal life produced the spider-and-fly.

Celibacy—the leopard.

The lion was always mighty but the cat could be capricious. S/he chose, therefore, to be the force for history as poetry.

                        From poetry we learn to be the pupil of the other.

Amongst *The Bestiary* beasts, cats are fabled most for being seers.

Vole

Sky is rising, ground is stiff—
       resistant—and the night a die.

I've reached a ring on the cedar: one old
       wound I have to work around

& wind in the white syringa
       throwing voices of the folk.

April flicks its split tongue out > a surcharge
       and it jars. Wherever there's air,

there's chugging and shunting;
       breath, the howl between. It's cold,

a vole comes in from it > beat;
       crawls like a baby, into your boot.

Stays there, safe, till you stick your foot in—
       it's not a foot to him but a club

that comes so fast it all looks
       black to the mammal.

       —Since you ask, he isn't crushed.
We fling him out, alive, to the dust.

       Before he scuttles under the brush,
I'm sure I hear the gnashing of miniature teeth.

Grenade

I smell your replica, *sitra achera*, shadow overlording dusk—
your favourite time of day. The whole night spread before you,
door ajar. I sense my shoulder tightening, from the teres muscle
up. Your fruit-fly eyes descending and those digits—canny as
bats'. I feel your spin and think of ants and spider-legs on flags.

A word escaped me yesterday. Its image came up vaguely in the
painting I was painting and I aimed to put it graphically in black.
Instead I shaped a pomegranate ~ shattered. Rudiments of colour,
split & spilt. I hit the floor, exasperated—curled up, knees-to-
nose; couldn't bring myself to rise for the door-chime;

saw in mind a man outside, standing at the portico, clutching
a delivery—my husband's power-pack. I set myself a *quid pro quo*:
If I recall that AWOL word, my husband gets his mail. The door-
bell chimes eleven times, the mailman is persistent. I stay lying,
down like Abel. Dumb in my bright red dress.

Metamorphoses

Some are born human, most have to humanize slowly.
I want to say I'm on my way > at this point: pelican;
in time, perhaps: writer. It seems every act of writing
is compensation for a shortfall of some sort; that to become
a writer one not only has to work hard at the part, but also
be a little less than human. Ideas like these weighed heavily
on Franz K. much of his truncated life. In fact, under their
anvil, he forged one of the few perfect works of poetic
imagination of the 20th century > according to Elias

Canetti. I don't wish to create the impression my mind
is turned wholly toward becoming other. I also peck at my
breast and reproach myself for succumbing, now and then,
to nihilistic piety. Mostly I've stayed upbeat in dark times—
satisfied to fish and fly. If, on occasion, I've felt the pull
of despair for having been bequeathed such an insignificant
tail, I'm grateful to have been compensated with a large
mouth-pouch and useful bill. Also with the vision to see:
my feathers moulting, over the open sea.

The Innocent Spin of Dreaming Real

I fell asleep on my elbow once and woke up
on a donkey that I rode into a monkey

sitting jauntily on its back. *See me as a rabbit,*
it said, believing it could speak:

The great thing is the no thing that is not,
it said repeatedly and threw me rudely off.

I think of monkey's rabbit and its 't'
becomes invisible, which shifts me to a city

with a wall where people come to wail
and pray and tuck their notes to God

into its broken gaps.
Once you said you were praying there—

forehead to the olden stone—
you glanced into a cranny and saw,

a mote or so from your nose, the wide eye
of a pigeon staring back. The hole in the wall

was big enough for a messenger bird, so scared
of you, it couldn't muster a single note. Or coo.

Spool

In the deep field where the spool people's
old moon sometimes succeeds in moving

bog waters in June — to flow over
wan weeds and make them gleam, we meet.

                                    Far out —
like migrant geese on evening's sleeve.

We've lost the notes but not the song,
which leaves as much on air as it lifts.

Your vaulting voice
is like the maundering moon in the meadow well —

there echo of December comes to drink.

Tammuz

We drove by dark in highwayed lights—

asphalt drawing us on, face-forward,

hard as hard-wired. Tents of trees, their

angles struck by glancing diamond-white.

Our narrow faces pale as newborn mice.

In the blued cool that fell as sunset

sank, we stopped talking > of the

fish dinner, the gallery visit. Hills

of pinkish dogwood at an inadvertent

turn. The coast hotel, its hallway smell,

sheets like gunwales and hulls. The message

stuck to the Monkey Puzzle: *It's alright to be*

troubled. The afternoon movie, analogous

hurt. Dark-descended made us see like chiefs.

Velocity Text

Flat seas, frozen axe.
The levelling force of vortex.
   Daughter, my laughter >
faster and faster.
   Stones blossoming,
      mammalling plants.
The man in my body com-
posing a poem > his fox-box.
   King bed.
      Velocity text.

Dreams demanding I give up sleep
that heaves me, harrowed, elsewhere—

Stoat approaching,   also crow, I'm

      at the window

slipping into thinness of erasure;

nothing in the foreground

presses back.

Fractals

She comes to the seaside, air-salts slick
　　　her skin like kith and kindling.
　　　　　　　　　　Runs, and needs to peak.
If she were an actor, she'd be the star kind—racing
and blazing away. A condition she can't really call being fit.

It happens that a man in a hot black suit
　　　　　　　　　　　　and high black hat,
　　　　　　　raises his voice as she passes:
Messiah, Messiah, Messiah, ai yai, yai-yai-yai-yai ...
　　　　　A crowd soon gathers, catching the tune,
　　　dancing like Rorschach and clapping.

How easily she runs, how concentrated. Eyes on the widening shoreline,
sinews glinting,
　　　　　　levity, levity ...

Anxious cats and mongrel dogs—

　　　　　　　　　　　at first she thinks they're pets.

Then the bigger visions and the voices—grand
　　　　　　　　and crashing.

　　　　　　　　Crumpled tickets, scribblings, clippings—
things that can't be thrown out now
　　　　　because they weren't thrown out before.

　　　Summer done and scuppered.

Down from treetops: leaves, the upper branches bare and airy,
bottoms—heavy yellow.

All the trunks upright, but one—
split into recurring curves,
diagonal across the ground
and sodden with September.
Time, we hope, will pardon the view;
time, as only
a spiral can.

A Panegyric

The pursuers withdraw to the citadel,
relieve their arms of upward gesture.

Dusk descends,
they lower their heads as well.

Kneel and keen for the people.
Violet skies reflect the forfeit;

wine-yellow moon, a truth.
They suffer sleep like hellcats

hounded; dream, as part of the penalty,
they'll not raise arms again.

At daybreak sun is storming orange.
Three effects, announce the solar seers,

will ravage the planet:
protons at careening speeds

will seize communications; mass coronal
plasma crash the electromagnetic

band; radiation inundate the planes.
To speak of sun, they say, is to embrace

its oscillations. Swaying like their leis,
they let the limpid vision lift them —

three eyes on the blazing rose,
three eyes on the binding.

The Stunt Bear, the Bell Tree

The landscape is loaded. Cluttered with bats and beer halls—
bats wrapped so the hands don't slip while swinging.
Beer halls—darts and pool. She lifts a mirror to her face,

stares into those deep blue pools. Streetlights pale as moons,
street moons. Air perfectly natural, naturally candid.
There are intervals of dark not even sun can interrupt.

Clouds—narrow, white as femurs—flowing over the city.
The secondhand keeps ticking away; the first: mute as meal.
Someone's rocking the barcarole, disrupting the dreamy dream.

Bathers, waiting for something to happen, look so glum
they could be shot. Many have fallen this way.
Many more have acted maniacally happy to save their lives—

only to end them later because they'd survived.
Find her while there's time—before the exits
shift. The stunt bear with the bell tree is exposing his tinny teeth,

the engine of his body chugging up. Rage rising, bells
revelling, inner fire bright.
Anyone who's broken down knows how savage health can be.

Quadriptych

Come midnight friends fill up the bar. Everyone has at least eight faces.
All fascinating. Changing places. Agitated as tadpoles,
like salamanders > from fire. Lickety-splitting through the night.
As day sinks in, the music moults,

the facets all collapse.
Slender on a chesterfield & smoking between two windows.
The smoke sucks into a cross-breeze
onto the city you resent [its architecture, traffic, false topography].

They want to say something, the exhalations.
But only moan.
Heart — dark and quartered,
old smoke low in the ventricle.

She does not know birds, yet there comes a day.   Canary,
like the way it sounds. Mellowing the cock's crow yellow,
airmail to coal-shaft black. Eyes follow the song to a slip on a clothes-
line, ash on the banister. When no one is looking, she laughs.

Lo

Trumpeter swans from Russia south for winter: En Bōqeq.
         What I see is food for what I see.
Mind meandering far from body,
                  over the dead and heavy sea
whose salt once healed an ugly summer cut.

Before the gush, the skin was insular—all the hexes
sealed. Trumpeter swans, their hearty honks.
Beyond them monumental mountains—Mo'av in the mist.
The gist of it—whatever rises
outside gets reflected
back. The terrace lit with candle-lanterns, oleander, jazz.
Lo, behold—
             the blue-note horns are us.

What I feel is food for what I feel.
I wish I could have swept you up, before the fall,
and ferried you away. The way the very air has weight,
the way you were a seraph once (when I was being razed)—
      light as light, insubstantial as grace.

Rain

Outside and inside are both intimate—they are always to be
reversed, to exchange their hostility.
    —Gaston Bachelard

Night after night, when I was a child, I belly-registered rain.

I woke in the dark to the inside sound of water. A sound

like drowning, steadily desperate, proximate, and wet.

I lay awake for hours—holding tight to my pyjama pants.

If the bed was moist, I could be sure the rain was real.

My sister, who slept through every weather, never seemed

to feel it: the thick dark shame of nighttime and insideness.

Ouija Board

I was slaked like a calf at the teat last night,
perhaps because the stars were low, so
low their leaky light suffused the garden.

This morning I was parched. Puppy dug a
backyard hole, your wallet gone from where
you put it, lying on the earth beside the digger

and the vinca. Puppy on the sofa gnawing rawhide
with a grin. She nuzzles you, she whimpers and
a word like squirrel drips as spittle from her

ruddy tongue. We leave her with the fish and walk
to the pond. I tell you, Spring will be benign—
umbilical, like love. Rain has made a Ouija Board

of dark allusive letters on the path. I pull the planchette
back. Which means no automatic talk, no plotting.
I mean, we're here, extemporizing, slipping into

mist the scent of daffodils and grass. We pause
before the water and our breath turns into breeze.
I tell you, Spring will be benign—resilient, I want this.

A sister is beside herself, beside the flimsy scrim of self,
impinged by force so strong it hogs her body. Eyes
complexly deadpan and it's not enough to look

to glyphs and sigils on the sidewalk, not enough
to love. I pull you close to view the yellow centres
of the celandine, the umbel of the primula, mucilaginous

leaves of the scilla set in a basal rosette. None of us
is too immune, no one too secure. Hounds come
bounding out of the brush. One dog sniffs the other's

rear, the first returns the favour. On the common
at the corner, geese have seized the green. A gander
wields his brawny bill and charges at your arm.

Instinctively you grab a branch and whack him
on the back. He hobbles to the pond and goes
berserk. We watch the mallards scatter and you cede

your piece of tree.   Think of some benignity ...
Sky is bluer higher up, and deeper—ultramarine. Lighter
by the horizon. Transparent as it eases into nearness.

Update on Nearness

We mirror the windows' panes and breaks.

Moon comes through; we take it as the great big pill it is—

in swallow-position, standing up.

Then shrink—heads first,

legs next. Our middles balloon to bobble-bellies.

These are the bodies we wanted > yes.

Also the gender and sex.

We got the parents we wanted as well;

even arranged the marriage from our choir invisible seats.

It was a bad match—

just what we needed for genes and growth.

Every night I go for a walk, I fall for the same black shadow.

Altarpieces

Someone's scraping blue-green off the moon—

must be the star-man,

rubbing till his points—all five—are rounded, worn to nubs.

Cut me flakes from serviettes: The thinner the paper

the quicker it yields to scissors.

O, says the flake, *how open the holes,*

Punctilious the Cutter: All the snippets on the table

sacrificed for form—

a copy of a copy of a copy unto thee.

The knight, on bended knee,

requests the principessa's hand. She yeses in solemnity

then afterwards laments the given fingers;

he, the bent patella.

An aura emanates from every statuette produced,

like breeze or shining light before a seizure ~

Azimuth

The wind that whistles over the outcrop, over the water,
ferries—through the cumulus—limbless figures:
      buoyant enough to bear their weight and sail.

It is as though a world subsists
             below them—copper-coloured,
                    blue and buff.

In a painting they'd be heading
west (from a viewer's point of view).
      In a map, north would be 'up', right
would be clockwise; west, by convention,
left.

        In a lifeline,
    they'd be sailing
back to the past, azure passing through their breeze-borne bodies
like a plane.

It is like them to be fixed and flying.

Smell the air.
    It must be
the copper chrysanthemums in the pot on the counter-top,
        because it couldn't be that shade of the shapes
           in the painting,
in which light is transacted, abstracted by life.

air

If you can accept air, you can accept beings of air;

you can accept the shadow

air holds in its nothingness and its light.

Easy, almost, as breathing. Easy as turning

your gaze from sun.

Easy as leaning and needing.

Easy as baby faces and the traces

left by loves. Easy as the still in the eye of the twister.

I call you, airy beings, I don't need to see to feel.

Most of what is real is immaterial.

Thin Girl

Thin girl says, If the shoe fits it's stiletto. Stilettos make the leg look lither.

Thin girl stands by the big girls in the shower at the gym, watching the water stroke her skin & bones.

She wonders if she'd be more loveable if her hair were longer ...

Some guy shouted Badass on the street the other day. Thin girl heard it Fatass and was sure he was aiming to scathe her.

Thin girl cannot *not* see the word *thin* in thinking.

She keeps a large selection of deodorants and colognes > atomizers only. She buys them for their mist.

Thin girl doesn't believe in diets, only in states-of-mind.

She'd like to become a mother, feel her womb contract and breasts reduce to prunes with every feeding.

She worries about getting pregnant,

lies on her yoga mat, monitors the flatness of her abdomen;

closes her eyes, envisions the spines of compact volumes of poems—

thinness as a metaphor for purity & plenty.

Secretly she purges.

Once upon a time, thin girl's mother was underweight: that became the standard. Thin girl fears she can't be under enough.

Voluptuous is an insult.

Thin girl lies awake at night, gazing into thin air—   give her this.

She's scared of losing reason for being;

conjures the power of opposites, coconut-oiled from toe to neck & rapt in a padded blanket.

Meridian

She went to the middle and sang out, as if music

were moving through her. A bright ebullient stream.

Almost at once, a circle surged. Upright, like people.

This is amazing, I thought. Who would believe it?

A circle moving like humans. And as they go round

they keep going. Like *Row Row Row Your Boat.*

But this is not the song. What she sang is a

mystery to me — blend of circle and girl.

∞

The hip kids are moving to the moon. On the way

they get star-tracked and never reach the moon.

One of the mothers, staring up at the stars, thinks,

I am lost in thought. The sky, fixed in her gaze, does

not alter. Yet comets come crashing, one after another,

down. This must be a miracle, she says. Or else a miracle.

Somewhere in the distance, they burn out. How typical.

How temporal. How utterly past adjustment.

∞

Sometimes he would light a fire and feed it.

Then continue on his way—leaving it to others.

Sometimes it would be a romantic lamp, lighting

the way for others to add value. Sometimes it

would fizzle out. Other times it would feed on itself

and the heat became so fierce everything overhead

caught fire. Then the others would come rushing

with their canisters and blankets to muster some.

∞

The weather is set. The crocuses in your nosegay

precede you like an explosion. Your heart wriggles

like fish in your ribs. I almost feel it leaping. You

come bubbling—your thoughts speech-balloons

around your head. I look into them and see myself

missing in every one. Now I'm looking away, thinking

of the fuselage shining like a fascinator. And you

inside lightning, balancing guesswork and trust.

∞

We would leave the room, into the woods, devour the

hour like wolves. Extend fast forelegs, disfigure private

anxieties hunkering down. This was safe when we were

puzzled about positioning—embankments giving way,

horizons sliding. Tribute must be given to the clarity

of accident prevention regulations, the supervisory ring

of clocking-off. We would bump along, double back.

Everything we said or kept bore the fuggy mug of juvenilia.

∞

We came to the lake at dusk. A euphony quickened

the willows—they moved to it, weightless and fey,

like sylphs. They moved to it fluidly, like undines.

You responded, too, sliding your hand along my sleeve—

as in the days you steered my arm in dance. Night

drew nigh, a tide in your eyes. I looked into the medium,

saw a bier—a catafalque, which seemed for a time like

the cottage-skiff to me, coming to take us out for a row.

∞

One night while the others slept, I climbed the roof

to the turret and sat like a crow under a night sky

strewn with dippers and hunters and queens —

their lights like bits of loose white lace tossed up.

I sat there, perched like a crow on the turret —

imagined myself on the ground looking up at the

crow. The nearness — the propinquity — of crow

as self and other made me eager to hear us speak.

∞

I felt for a while the sky was mine: the moon,

the stars, the indigo wind; sun's pale circle

rising at the horizon. The whole countryside

pulsed with the hum of becoming. *We're finishing,*

it whispered into the distance. Then to the greater

distance it whispered, *We're not.* The ending word

returned to be retold. After seven — eight — the

lemniscate. Shadow at the crossover point and curves.

∞

Promontory

Some things you can never hold:
The whorl that reels behind your eyes.
Vision—
        a majestic alternate future.
Glimpsed through sinusoidal lids.
Otherwise at sea and fed by tempest. Tint & tone.

No white to speak of
back of blindness. What to hear but *rush*.
                         Bridge de-
taching from the isthmus. Thunder in the tint,
or is it lightning, close to tone ...
I close my eyes

and lean against the architrave—the door—
trying to decide which shade of grey
dusk becomes.
           Below the open window, sea is
calling to the rock, *Wonder yonder, promontory.*
Only don't go down.

A stream of naked people—holding torches,
tambourines—is marching through the dark
toward the shore.
          As they disengage,
their music merges with the surge.
Their torches rise to daimons on the water.

Elemental

Sometimes as I'm being sad, attending to
the plant that stands for thanks,
a wind comes swinging from the east,
calling and mocking me, hollowly.

I want to know the ovenbird in the forest
by its rustle. The way you know my
footfall by its echo through the house,
even when you're sitting on the deck.

She's lying still — a temple window —
diamond of her life beneath the sheets.
Now and then light-breath ascends,
into the shade above the bed.

She claims to see the beings in the upperparts:
Believe her.
Their evening glow
and adumbrated wings.

Lithium was in the beginning,
elementally light. Its salts have happened
down to us as remedy for depression.
We slept by the black-dog

pond, imagining happiness,
and lifted. Among the souls who love
the great ineffable shape of the name,
one would be Odette.

Think of a Name for the Bird in the Glossy Photo

Do we name her for her coat—Red Ruby, Black Cape,
Turquoise Sleeve? Or for the bow of her beak,

the blade of her tail? Do we name for her
compact body? Better—for her call:

If she has the gift, her song will surely
mimic crystal ringing past the shadow

sun throws over the folds.
You have to imagine, that's the task.

It's time to put your pride aside, dis-
card everything heavy. Even your thinness.

Your eyes, their saturated blue,
too steeped in hue to really look. Yet you do.

You turn to me in your opulent gloom
and I see you don't want to be soothed.

This is not unusual. How many times
have you turned away, how many times

have I opted for the garden, or for art.
Even now at 2 a.m. I'm upstairs at my table

shaping photos, notes, and pieces of paintings
into a new collage. I bring you up

from the basement and you say, Okay,
okay. I like the way your voice accedes,

the way you quip, Ideas come from air.
I think we know in this moment

I will crawl across the world for you,
in and out of the demon's mouth,

through the thick of his haunch,
to make you safe. But now we're naming.

Everything Reminds You of Something Else

The steady is a pneumatist, a producer—tech house music.
Therefore electronic; mix. The girl from Ben-Yehuda
tucks her torso into a tube-top, plucks her leg hair one by one.
Files her nails to tapers, paints the pinkies white with lightning
strikes, texting with her index for protection. Numeral *ix*

at the foot of the page springs into a walking stick, lifts its
insect wings and flits away. In February life misfired ~ twisted
to misprision. Voices trespassed speech, surfaces failed colour.
Concrete disobeyed its physics, rioting against the walker's heels.
Outside-swinging-inside ~ pervious skin. Hardly held together.

Everything reminds you of something else. Moses shines
his light on the wilds, a great white rhino startles and stops >
a footfall from the jeep. Huge tube-head and hoary horns, just
high enough to touch. You snap a shot, he swerves and hurtles
bluntly into the brush. The image we had—until you removed it—
blur of the witness-primitive.

K.

You sang the ancient wail of the sad animal,
made it always modern.
Like infinite wind, the dark at dusk.—

elegant as number.
Gaunt blossom, hungry son:
got none of the food you liked and slowly starved.

Your gaze, the weight of slate and mail,
still vaster than *The Castle*—
Why did you arrive if not to remain ...

Never were you photographed in profile,
or behind—the back of your head,
bat thin-tip ears, thick horsehide hair:

I imagine. Absolute hands,
the vaporous
shade of your nails.

I sat at the hotel-chair you sat at,
set my arms upon the desk;
could not procure a word.

But the wood that beat in the heart
of the wood is the same brown
grain that touched your palms and paper.

Isn't it felicitous—this furniture, this silent set—
was spared as fire rained the sky,
flattening more than half that city to ash.

Hohner

I keep the object
in the lacquer box
where it's a hidden
man from a marine

band. Tucked against
the dark interior, its
effect on the velvet
is the stuff of high

mystery — how restraint
can be so maverick
its motionlessness
leaves notes.

The Man with the Perfumed Moustache

You wouldn't know the moustache was perfumed—
if not for the up-stretched neck of the woman,

sniffing it, smiling like Briar Rose. Nothing of the
unusual happens. But the man has held across his chest

a vintage ukulele. So you assume he plays the good
old tunes: *I've Been Working on the Railroad,*

*Camptown Races, Buffalo Gals Won't You
Come Out Tonight, Amazing Grace,*

America > which is the same as *God Save the Queen*
with different words. This alignment,

together with the veracious way the woman
conveys the rose-scent of that moustache, strikes me

as expertly metrical. It is a copacetic moment. I'm happy,
surprised I'm not happier …

Year of the Horse

I kissed him and he bit. I offered my pink little breast

and he fussed. —Who has never felt stunted?

The tongue, the tooth, the wing, the hoof:

any part could be of use. What animal,

do you reckon, would suction be the stomach of—

**

Men in cloaks across the street in single file at dusk. Rays

from somewhere underneath them bathe their benthic faces.

We came out from the gallery, the Guggenheim Exhibit. Perhaps

it was a Kupka, a Kandinsky, or Chagall—forces from those

halls that frayed the veil. Trees against the winter welkin—nerves

exposed and frozen. Smoke contorting into orbs of cinder-blue

pollution. We take to the car; I claim the passenger seat and yield

to sleep. There a tale unfolds in which the hero is a hole—the

gap he tumbles into. An aperture and lantern-like, Lamp Black.

Open as a nose and throat, hollow as a hose. Tubular and spooling

forward *warmth*—

***

Says, Here be Laxnes, here the stream. Ford it, take the acreage,

bend the breadth. Leaning in, I whisper in his ear, Don't heave me,

Long Nose. He's skittish as a kite-tail in an updraft. My gut assumes

the tilt of his fetlock tölting up the hill — alluvial-green, confettied

with pebbly pockets, matted grass. The half day-moon — diaphanous,

a cataract on azure. The river hardly ripples except when he snorts.

Says, Trolls be here, get ready, and the others kick up dust. My ride

slows to trot; dallies and I turn my cheek to the wet-sock neck of

his scent. A kittiwake lands on a branch; we view the rudimentary toe.

Wind trips over the matted grasses, slips behind a tree.

A drumming from the trunk, or is it Long Nose throwing his whinny.

There's no fill-in for the word horse.

Pony won't do, nor mule.   The herd is vanished, over the slope,

beyond the empty bend. The bend ascends and quickens now

we're siblings going back.

****

Max remains in his seat as the train approaches his destination.

That no one knows his whereabouts

appeals to his sense of sadness.

He smirks at the apparition in the window — it's himself,

imagining Franz Kafka

      might have sat in this very seat

and smirked at his own sad visage in the window

          decades prior.

A pain beneath his scapula shoots suddenly into his shoulder as

the wingtip of a jackdaw flaps his image in the glass.

He thumbs the knotty spot on his back and notes the synchronism:

He's always called that knot his 'wing-insertion'.

The sepia print shows W.G. (Max) Sebald and Franz Kafka sitting

in a train seat gazing out the window, Sebald superimposed on Franz —

like cumulus over nimbus. Kafka's wingtip ears project beyond the frame

of Sebald's face. A furtive smirk on both men's lips — like cirrus under stratus.

*****

Alone on the upper deck last night, I saw a flying saucer circle
       slowly over the ship. The giant iris blinked and winked away.

Years ago at En Harōd, lying on a grassy slope, first night
in the country, I saw a thousand comets fall and fizzle into black.

I made a wish, then two, then ten ...   finally cried all night.
Afterwards I learned they are an annual phenomenon.

But timing, at the time, made them miraculous, a pivot.
As January turns her back, maybe the chronomantic

sign is light. The moon and stars are merging
and their shadows > great white hoofs.

Horse and Ride Her

Perhaps between whinnies: ennui,
press of the tether &
extra weight—
maybe another mount.

A bridle and veil for the naked
lady sailing through a druid-
blue. There's only so much
the angels can do—

Who will rescind the redundancy,
open the fetlocks,
unshoe the hooves?
Even now as you've forestalled

falling in order not to follow
the rule, you find yourself
slipping & losing your grip.
Even on this flattened palette

hind limbs trail away,
saddles thin to invisible
and the mist is a tryst
of bliss and swindle.

Cord

First the forces: gases, heat and radiation;
stars. *We are stardust*
sing the physicist and bard.

We are quartz and bats and roses,
we are poetry: Brock-Broido, Blake.
Baudelaire, Bidart.

We're fugue of Bach and Glass; Celan.
World gets into us every breath.
Yes to every sentence.

I held to the imbecile cord ~ till it ripped.

When the diagnosis arrived,
we flew to a city of history and art,
visited galleries, stood before works

that made a life look edgeless.
The paintings I looked at longest were the Turner
waterscapes: ships and mists, conflating waves ~

wild violets and yellows, flaming grey.
Creaturely chaos. Suns, the seas.
And in my mouth: the froth.

Theory of Dreaming

The garden
my solace, especially in winter: plants
detach and snow
obliges stone.

I sit at the window alone,
insular as January.
Still.

The trees have a static quality too, like stars,
though slowly, very slowly becoming Suns.
Their thin limbs radiating outward.

Lifetimes pour before me.
Here I sit awaiting a car, there awaiting the war.
A shepherd,
then a girl with a hump, like mother.
But more like sister: we're twins.
She the lighter; I the dark and heavier;
she the fey ~

The air outside is thick with beings —
vertical in falling snow.
Close as claustrophobia,
though not confined to the garden.

Maybe they're angels. If so,
what is their message —
Is it that if I live on, I become a figment of one?

And is it actually January, or am I already gone?

Perhaps we all are angels.
          And have given up our flesh,
and are no longer free.

Oculus

Curtain of the firmament, tin-stars punched in for glitter

and the moon a yellow oculus, the sun a holy ghost. Spectres ~

in from everywhere ~ diaphanous as gas, their traces shaping/

shifting into gist. Grouped among the returnees,

                                        I'm landing.

Image of the children leaping, squealing as they see me and the pinwheel

spinning in the breeze, the beech, its ruby leaves. The children leaping

on the lawn—the lima-bean green grass toward me. Beaming, I am

flashing shiny teeth in hot-pink lips. Love me, says the bliss, it's

unashamed to be exuberant. And they, as yet too young to feel

fatigued by such enthusiasm, leap across the boggy lawn.

      Image of the children leaping, splashing in the

puddle-mud and springing high-5-faced toward me,

croaking from the rosy toads of their throats:

Catch us, Savta, lift us up. Spin us ~ jump ~

                    jump up

Summer

Waiting for the solstice
                    for the voodoo lily to bloom.

In the low light of dusk
clouds blue enough to cover grey

come grazing over the maples. Like macrocosmic sheep.
The season of expanding and dissolving into cosmos.

Once when we were falling
apart, you argued time was on-side.

We waited for the voodoo to bloom: snake palm,
stink lily, dragon arum;

                    missed it.
By Friday it had shrivelled to a black amorphophallus.

This dried up stiff was it.
Like macrocosmic sheep

the clouds came grazing, bluish grey—
                    unstated over maples. It seemed

once we were falling
apart: You argued time was on-side.

Which meant—I see now—
neither of us could fade away

          or bail.

Burnt Bridge

The creek receives from drainage ditches, spigots, dirty rain.
Water quality ranges > poor to worse. The first bridge, built in
1895, returned to ash. Skulls in the cellar next to the Writers'

Cottage by the creek. African natural history hung on walls,
displayed in cases. Taxidermied guinea fowl, invertebrates
and lizards; a zebra head & neck. The spectre of a former

tenant hovers in the halls. It's said she makes her presence
felt in switches. *Pull your feet up into your knees, knees up
into femurs. Fold your shoulders into your ribs, upper and*

lower limbs to the visceral middle. You're ready, good to go —
Over the harlequin glorybower, clerodendrum, myrtle. Past the
feral clematis and cardoon, its mauve capitulum. The everyday

at your front and flanks. The past > that doesn't back off. Every-
where the metaphor. The burning bridge, the limns, the feet —
by these you'll find a lead. Creek meandering into the opaque

lake. Sink your soft soles into the soil above the rocky water,
swish your tunic-linen with the wind. Lie beneath the gunnera
like a nymph and yield to sleep: There the key > in dreams.

That zebra sporting forelegs off the wall. Sun-saddle. Moon-
mantle. Odradek stars — whatever those are. Dark zipped into
them neatly, and deleted.

Riding to Ronda

What can be remembered,
what made up —

The unsure eye
slips this to that
in landscape past the bus-glass.
Trees stream into helio
ceiling / sky
flipped into ground. A pond dissolves to
leafless / greenish
clouds the stuff of cotton-floss   flung up.

      When Noah had had enough of one dull colour
he dispatched the dove.
She brought him back an olive branch; next sortie
she vanished —
           out of form > disorder

or these clouds forever morphing — swan to dog
to donkey, Don Miguel and Dulcinea;
Sancho Panza's staff (for he had once commanded sheep),
to high white turbines.

And Rilke wrote in Elegy Six of *urge to action,*
rivering air; of Samson, how his destiny
was buried in his breast. When he smashed those pillars,
he burst out of the force of flesh, *into a narrower*
world where he went on choosing …

I recall deciding
         at the stony lip of a bridge —
singularly beautiful and Romanesque, like Ronda's.

Or was this only in a poem ...
or had I already leapt?

And was it into water after air, or into arms?
        And didn't you not let on,
for the sake of subtlety,
        my heaviness —

Belt of Living Things: a zodiac suite

i

The shepherd stows a blade in his belt. His soles click
like the rock-bottom of hooves as he climbs >
fired up from the field. The mountain that supports his test will become
hub of inordinate struggle.
Best of love, he says to his young son—bound and ready for death.
To the surrogate he says nothing. The ram,
whose one big task is sacrifice, yields to the shepherd's knife,
giving the man a long and human look.

ii

Even burned the earth is firming, grasses fielding green.
          The oxen, slow in their yokes, forge on, turn at the verge >
return.
Where does such stubbornness come from?
                                        Or is it not stubbornness
so much as commitment to symmetry, instinct for the physical ...
There's something incomparably soft about these bulls:
their horns like painted nails of elegant women.

iii

The artist who also writes is a double-double.

The mere routine of writing, says Peg, splits a human in two.

iv

We cede our heavy legs to the rubbery suits like buoys on a float,
the sponginess of our lungs to the thinness of living; swim by the
skin of our fins past puffers and grunts to blue-footed boobies.
Your flipper touches mine and we are turtles for a time—

I wondered, as we stepped from the deck, onto the back
of the Zodiac: What relation does the booby
                              bear to the Sally Lightfoot Crab?
The tortoise to the cormorant, the dolphin to the albatross,
the Fernandina mouse to Darwin's finch?

And does the starry hunter hold the pointer in his sword ...

v

Kafka noted in his diary one Léonie Frippon—a dancer in a cheek-
to-cheek red dress. Long lashes, limber limbs, a massively curly up-do.
"She sang 'Button Collection in the Louvre.'" (Who knew?)

            At what point is something completely gone?
The last of the sunlight stunning as it sinks a solar flare. Come closer. Stare.

vi

Wholly you know the proficient one who exacted flesh and untouched it.
It will come to this: immaculateness, beauty-diffuse.
Innocence of chemistry / of colour / of the electromagnetic spectrum.
Hale and all hallow.

vii

Once, I happen to know, you made a poppet from a stocking
and gave it my name, which you mispronounced. You gave it
my height and weight as well and stitched it exactly to scale.
Not so much to shrink me, I think. More for the sake of balance.
Then stuck it—half with needles, half with pins.

viii

I was a pushover for a plinth: I stood him up for a pillar
who looked heavenly on a pedestal. High and mighty, classic as acanthus.
He told me he could keep it up.
It's truer to say I needed him to—

                without the verticality we'd be shattered.
Which is why I say of behaviour, *Beautiful is as beautiful does;*
of scorpion*s, Hyperbole*; of marriage, *Whatever you bring to it
you get.*

ix

Wind moves through the room, inflecting your breath. Like nothing
we've ever seen the corkscrew hazel flexes its chest. Spots on your legs
are copies of constellations: bear and archer, the queen. Noon sky stretches,

                drops its cloth. The green of every needle
separates: It's harder and harder to keep this shade in place. Look at your weight >
way down where you thought it could never conceivably get. I'm sensing
your restlessness, though restlessness isn't exactly the right semantic.

x

Weeds of the field stock-still as frost. White as lumen and lux.
The heavens bleating flecks.   A mountain goat
ascends at dawn, leaping through the nimbus, light's jug of milk on his pelage,
snow in his coat. He holds to higher notes (as in Shadrach is Hananiah).
And on his breast—   a locket
taking off.

xi

The water shows its shape in coiling colour:
aureolin yellow, phthalo turquoise, iridescent greens.
Sound as if from light transmutes from pulse to hum to melody—
a tune as fine and unalloyed as foam.
The water-carrier *slips his Mind.*
Sun is up and for a moment—omen: tinkle, babble, wings and bells, ker-
plop, a frog's first sigh. The tiny muffled
plunk of honeybees landing. Flowers furling, ants parading to pass.
                    Mind his slips—
the carrier is Mistress of Reversals.

xii

Ash-tree yellow, leaves the shape of *vesica*
            piscis, swimming fish.
Upward in the trunk: sap's tacit descant.
The spooks would flee to the fields.
If they were free, they'd leave me too, die and rest forever.
I was sick, they visited and assembled
and dissembled, came tapping at my breastplate
from the stretches and the depths;   I trembled for the centre.
Everybody takes the shape of un-
becoming something.
I didn't have to worry that the children wouldn't love me; they didn't
have to worry I would leave.
            The cichlids in the tank continue
swimming even as they sleep—
gazing, like the faithful,
with their wall-eyes   and their eye-shine.

November on the Cusp of Archer

It is a dark day, the
ground grey.
I'm waiting
at the window for a portent to appear.

A squirrel
exits the hedgerow,
picks a nit from his coat
and bolts.

      I've put you in the picture again.
           (Is there another word for 'thirst'?)
      I need a term that will hold me open.
              (How about 'aporia'?)
      Sun like a ring, like a noose.

There was a boy
in middle school
who drew in class all day.
Drawings of tiny airplane pieces—
nuts and bolts of wings and motors,
fuselages, cargo—
breaking up from some imagined

                        impact

He drew with unbelievable speed and surgical
precision—picture after picture of dis-

                integrating planes.

He left before the end of term.
          We never exchanged a word.

I've kept a mental image of his gaze:

Cuy

Guinea-pig whole and splayed on the plate.
The room they put you down in
bright, table-banter light.
The chef from the winter tour group,
his fork in your neck
and knife at your thigh, can laugh:
His wife is wearing a Tilley hat.
My gut's a mess and there is no taking it out.

In Ottawa, the rabbit Jasper sleeps on a pine-
chip bed in the den, dines on lettuce & pellets.
Jasper is a virgin and a bachelor, like a man.
Originally he was Julie, till he grew.
The other four-legged—Pat the cat—
fell (or leapt) from the tenth floor ledge
and lived. We found her in the shrubbery,
given back, but different. Whether

we're *apprentice to the common law of harm*
or not, we feel it. Pat flicks her tail and licks
her coat, dips her tongue in the water bowl,
yet never appears to eat. This is her capacity now,
her vision. I think of this in Otavalo, cuy's ex-shape
on the plate. Cuy in a field, complete somewhere,
restored and incorporeal. Gathered to her species again,
Decembering—

Strand

Love is not a word that comes amenably from my mouth.
It stalls at the palate, or further back—in the brain,
at the hippocampus. Someone was saying something

about the system and booming through it, the bobbing
waters & falling under their spell; that conchs are shellfish
coffins for whispered wishes of human beings, or beings

costumed as humans, with fingers and feet. The foot,
this someone said, is seat of the soul, the heel the wheel.
I'm sensitive to tropes like these. Everything reminds me

of something else. And I've got this plantar fasciitis—
have had it for months, in my deep left heel. Left,
this someone said, is the side of the feminine, & of love.

It rankled me to hear this and my hand shot up to the sore
on my upper-left lip. I didn't need to look in a mirror
to see it, but when I did, I noticed the raw red crater

was stuck with a strand of tissue or fluff ~ fluttering
like a tiny wayward angel.   —Where was the breeze?
This someone mentioned stars as well—in a tone I wanted

to keep but it seeped to the ethers. The stars that stayed
remind me of this image of my inner breasts ~ watery digital
constellations marked with ink-black holes the doctor called cysts.

World Light

We watch the seventh episode — I'm buffered. People
on the screen inhabit the room, continue my thinking. I

step out onto the deck, the dark. The unequivocal snow.
I could be shocked and traumatized, but not killed off mid-

plot — I'd have to survive till the season wraps, at least.
I watch my breath curl into cold, enfold the falling flakes;

picture the two of us in bed, midnight quiet as rime.
You're rolling the flannel blanket between your thumb

and index finger like an infant in his crib. I'm reading to you —
a Nordic story. Same thick book I've been reading to you

for years. You know it's about a poet yet you never remember
his name. Enough to hear my voice and feel my foot against

your calf. I wriggle and puff the blanket up; you grunt
and flatten it back, complain that I am letting in the cold.

Maybe it's so. We've generated rituals — soft drugless soporifics.

— These might be signs as well by which we'll recognize each other
in a deeper future sleep: There is no light where that is, so we're eyeless.

And Somewhere in the After-Image Winged Creatures Tread Gently on the Soft Ground

The mountainsides—let's say the sides—depicted bitumen black.
Brown debris and blackened scraps of golden shadow-facets.

The face of the cave—let's say a cave—gigantic black and slick.
The canopy above it, ashen; floor—a River Styx.

Knives of light can't part the dark that concentrates the hidden.
I stand before the image with my one good eye, my one good hand—

its bluish veins like subcutaneous creeks;
gaze conjunctively into the blood, the hand becomes a map.

Eventually
the differences collapse:

body is the starry sky, artifice the spark. The murderer the murdered
and the fugitive the found; the audience, the living-piece performed:

Our hearts are in the darkness, our hearts are in the chest.
Metered to the spheres and set to music.

Choir

My name is Leo Kleiner and my zaideh was a mason
who hewed griffins for an Edmonton hotel. I was baptized

Ralph bin Williams till I switched it. I lie with a ghost of

Kafka's past. His Hebrew name was Anschel—meaning angel—
and his double was a monk. It won't be eiderdown my wings

will fill with, not I of partial parents bred. I'll gather

stiffer feathers from the nests of jays and ravens, bind them
like a writer with the help of Strand and Glück, stitch them

to my back with invisible silk. Invisible: the father of me

and I against my mother: tree. The name I take takes me.
And when from me my form is freed, the name will be included.

Walking Song

I hold my fingers to the rain. It would drench them anyway,
even in my pocket. Cool-as-pewter bindi on my lip.

You are where I'm walking to. The song of you is all along,
the name the same, again. You are rock—the walrus—strong

and oblong by the pond. You the thin birch-limb reflected
wet, the flagstone path. You the handle on the gate, the lattice

and the lantern. You the red ranunculus—medicinal, the tincture.
You the espalier beneath the yew and pyracantha. You

the door, the portico. The jamb. When I get back, I'll shed my
shoes and hang my coat to drip. You are where I'm walking to,

and always. You the rock—the walrus—strong and oblong, song,
the name, again. Now a second finer rain is falling on the first.

Notes

Metamorphoses: In *Kafka's Other Trial: The Letters to Felice*, Elias Canetti writes that in *The Metamorphosis* Franz Kafka "had written something he would never surpass, because there is nothing that could possibly surpass *The Metamorphosis*, one of the few great and perfect works of poetic imagination written during this century" (Schocken Books, 1974:20).

Tammuz: The Hebrew lunar month that corresponds to July. For my mother.

Grenade: *"sitra achera"* is Aramaic for the "other side"—the evil inclination in Jewish mystical literature. The word for "grenade" in Hebrew is the same as the word for "pomegranate": "rimōn"—the word that escapes the narrator in the poem.

Update on Nearness: Conceived under the title "Needy" in response to Susie Petersiel Berg's poem "After John Massey" in *How to Get over Yourself* (Piquant Press, 2013:61) for *You Will Still Have Birds, A Conversation in Poems* (A Lyricalmyrical Handmade Book, 2015).

Oculus: For Leah, Judah, and Ami.

Burnt Bridge: In Franz Kafka's short story "The Cares of a Family Man," "Odradek" is a mysterious star-shaped spool with an inextinguishable creaturely aspect. For Ann and Warren Howard, in whose Writers' Cottage the poem was drafted.

Riding to Ronda: The italicized phrases are from David Young's translation of Rainer Maria Rilke's "Sixth Elegy" in *Duino Elegies* (W.W. Norton & Company, 2006:115,117).

Cuy: Guinea pig (pronounced "coo-ee"), a traditional food of Andean people. The line *apprentice to the common law of harm* (italicization mine) is from Lucie Brock-Broido's poem "In Owl Weather," in *Stay, Illusion* (Alfred A. Knopf, 2013:35).

Strand: Owes a debt of gratitude to the poetry of Canadian born, American poet Mark Strand (1934-2014).

Choir: Inspired by Robert Pinsky's poem "Chorus" which appeared in *The New Yorker*, February 5, 2015:55.

Acknowledgements

I am grateful to the editors of the following publications in which these poems originally appeared, some in different renditions:

The Antigonish Review: "Horse and Ride Her," "Choir"

The Boneshaker Anthology: "Quadriptych," "Elemental"

Canadian Literature: "Velocity Text," "And Somewhere in the After-Image Winged Creatures Tread Gently on the Soft Ground"

Canthius Literary Journal: "Cuy"

Contemporary Verse 2: "Jerusalem Day"

The Dalhousie Review: "The Bower," "The Innocent Spin of Dreaming Real," "Strand"

Descant: "Hohner"

Dr. William Henry Drummond 2014 Spring Pulse Poetry Festival Anthology: "Walking Song"

Echolocation, The Chase Chapbook Contest: "Fractals," "A Panegyric" —**First Place**

Event poetry and prose: "Metamorphoses," "Tammuz," "Everything Reminds You of Something Else"

FreeFall Magazine: "Promontory"

The Impressment Gang: "Rain," "Altarpieces"

The Junket (UK): "Theory of Dreaming," "Riding to Ronda"

Kestrel, A Journal of Literature and Art (US): "Spool"

Levelerpoetry.com (US): "Lo," "World Light"

The Maynard: "Thin Girl"

Nashwaak Review: "The Bestiary," "Air," "Burnt Bridge," "Belt of Living Things: a zodiac suite," "November on the Cusp of Archer"

One Word at a Time: Poetry and short stories from the 2011 gritLIT competition: "Meridian" — **First Place**

Prairie Fire: "Ouija Board," "Azimuth"

The Puritan: "Year of the Horse"

Shirim (US): *A Jewish Poetry Journal, Canadian Jewish Poetry Issue:* "Grenade," "K."

Taddle Creek Magazine: "The Stunt Bear, the Bell Tree"

Truck, halvard-johnson.blogspot.ca: "The Man with the Perfumed Moustache"

Vallum contemporary poetry: "Tower," "Cord," "Summer"

Warm thanks to The Long Dash writing group: John Oughton, Mary Lou Soutar-Hynes, Sheila Stewart, Yaqoob Ghaznavi, Clara Blackwood, and Merle Nudelman who have heard, read, and offered valuable feedback on many of the poems in this collection. Thanks to Susie Petersiel Berg, my indefatigable co-creator of the chapbook, *You Will Still Have Birds*, bound with care by the talented Mr. *Lyricalmyrical* himself, Luciano Iacobelli. Thank you, Luciano! Thanks to Steven McCabe for his electric illumination of my poem "Metamorphoses," on his site poemimage.

wordpress.com. Thanks to Conan Tobias for longstanding support of my work and for showcasing my poem "Think of a Name for the Bird in the Glossy Photo" on *The Taddle Creek Podcast*. Thanks to Elizabeth Greene and B.W. Powe for reading the final draft of my manuscript and offering gracious endorsements. There's no replacement for the comradeship of literary friends and colleagues.

Thanks to the Women's Art Association of Canada studio artists: Wenda Watt, Barbara Feith, Beryl Goering, Mary Lou Payzant, Wendy Weaver, and Judith Davidson-Palmer, whose art provided inspiration for the poems "Tower" and "Azimuth"; "The Bestiary"; "Air"; "Horse and Ride Her"; vignette *xi* of "Belt of Living Things: a zodiac suite," "And Somewhere in the After-Image Winged Creatures Tread Gently on the Soft Ground," respectively. And to WAAC studio artists Barbara Andersen, Carolyn Jongeward, Marjorie Moeser, and Gail Read, whose work over the years has also inspired ekphrastic poems.

Special thanks to publishers Connie McParland and Michael Mirolla for their commitment to Guernica Editions, to the Guernica staff for all their hard work on behalf of the house and its authors, to Guernica founder Antonio D'Alfonso for bringing me in to the fold in the first place and opening opportunities along the way, to Michael again for his generosity, keen editorial eye, and exceptional *menschlichkeit* in all dealings. And to David Moratto for the fabulous cover and interior design.

Deep gratitude to my family, especially my husband Menachem Wolff.

About the Author

Elana Wolff is the author of five solo collections of poems and a collection of essays. She has also co-authored with Malca Litovitz a collection of rengas, co-authored a chapbook with Susie Petersiel Berg, co-edited with Julie Roorda a collection of poems written to poets and the stories that inspired them, and co-translated with Menachem Wolff poems from the Hebrew by Georg Mordechai Langer. Her poetry has been translated into French and her poems and prose have garnered awards. She has taught English for Academic Purposes at York University in Toronto and at The Hebrew University in Jerusalem. She currently divides her professional time between writing, editing, and designing and facilitating social art courses.

Printed in December 2016
by Gauvin Press,
Gatineau, Québec